a Will

John Humphries

ESSENTIALS

Published in 2001 by
How To Books Ltd, 3 Newtec Place,
Magdalen Road, Oxford OX4 1RE, United Kingdom
Tel: (01865) 793806   Fax: (01865) 248780
e-mail: info@howtobooks.co.uk
www.howtobooks.co.uk

British Library Cataloguing in Publication Data.
A catalogue record for this book is available from
the British Library.

Edited by Francesca Mitchell
Cover design by Shireen Nathoo Design
Produced for How To Books by Deer Park Productions
Typeset by PDQ Typesetting, Newcastle-under-Lyme, Staffordshire
Printed and bound by Bell and Bain Ltd., Glasgow

ESSENTIALS *is an imprint of*
How To Books

Contents

Preface   **7**

1   **Why You Should Make a Will**   **9**
Who can make a will?   10
When a will can be made   11
The benefits of making a will   14
What happens if you do not make a will   15
The rules of intestacy   16
Problems caused by not making a will   19

2   **Writing a Will**   **22**
What can be included in your will   23
Who can benefit from your will   26
Methods of making a will   30
Who is involved   32
Constructing the will   34
Legal requirements   37

3   **Reducing the Tax Burden**   **40**
Inheritance tax   41
Property and other assets   41
Gifts   44
Trusts   48
Paying inheritance tax   50

4 Changing Your Will   **53**
Reasons for making changes   54
Making changes to your will   55
Challenging your will   56
Conditions   58
Disputes   61

5 Understanding Probate   **63**
The need for probate   63
How to apply for probate   65
The executors' duties   67

6 Other Types of Will   **73**
Making a will in Scotland   73
Military wills   76
International wills   78
Living wills   79
Powers of attorney   80

7 And Finally   **84**
Safeguarding your will   84
Keeping records   85

Appendix 1 Glossary   **88**

Appendix 2 Example of a simple will   **93**

Preface

Making a will is really a very simple matter, yet the majority of people in the United Kingdom die without leaving one. Dying without making a will or 'intestate', can cause unnecessary difficulties for those you leave behind. That is something I am sure nobody wants. The purpose of this book is to guide you step by step through the process of writing your will. It shows what you can leave to whom, how to reduce the burden of Inheritance Tax, how to avoid your will being contested after you are no longer in a position to explain your reasons and how to make things easier for your executors.

There is a chapter illustrating the differences between wills made in England and Wales and those in Scotland and another to help your executors to obtain probate. At the end of the book is a glossary of terms which you should find useful when talking to your solicitor.

I hope that this book takes the mystery out of wills and that as a result you will take that all-important step and make a will.

John Humphries

1 Why You Should Make a Will

Many people believe that making a will is equivalent to signing their own death warrant. Of course it is not. It is a common sense step to ensure an orderly disposal of your assets when you eventually die.

In this chapter, the six things that really matter:
~ Who can make a will?
~ When a will can be made
~ The benefits of making a will
~ What happens if you do not make a will
~ The rules of intestacy
~ Problems caused by not making a will

A will is a legal document setting out in detail how a person wishes their estate to be disposed of upon their death. It can be as simple as leaving everything to your next of kin or detailed to the point of nominating specific books to named people. Once written, a will is not set in stone, it can be changed at any time.

Who can make a will?

A will can be made by any of the following people:

~ Anyone over the age of 18 and 'being of sound mind'. This means that at the time of making their will they were fully aware of what they were doing. The will of anyone who is deemed insane under the Mental Health Act remains valid if they were sane at the time of making the will.

~ Military personnel under the age of 18 if on active service (see Chapter 6).

~ Foreigners with land or property in the United Kingdom who wish it to be disposed of under English law.

~ United Kingdom citizens living abroad.

When a will can be made

A will can be made at any time once the person has reached the age of 18. However, many people only make their will when there is a specific change in their personal life.

Marriage

A husband or wife is legally referred to as 'the spouse'. If you die without making a will, the surviving spouse automatically inherits all or the majority of your estate. Therefore, if you wish other people to also benefit, this needs to be specified in your will.

Live-in partners

It is now more common for couples to live together without getting married. However, 'common law' partners are not considered by the law to be spouses. Therefore, the surviving partner has no automatic claim on the estate of a partner who dies without making a will. It is necessary therefore to make provision for the surviving partner by means of a will. They must be named specifically in the will.

Divorce

If there is no will, the divorced spouse loses all rights to your estate. Should you wish your divorced spouse to benefit, this must be made clear in your will.

Children

Although your children, including illegitimate and legally adopted ones will benefit if you do not leave a will, you may want to make specific provisions for them. Step-children have no automatic rights to an *intestate* (not disposed of by a will) estate but can of course benefit from a will.

Hospitalisation

If you go into hospital for a major operation or are diagnosed with a serious illness, although hopefully the risk of dying is minimal, you may wish to put your affairs in order, by making a will.

Retirement

Approaching or reaching retirement is often the time when people decide to make a will.

You may believe that there are unlikely to be any major changes to your assets in the future, so now is the time to put your affairs in order by means of a will.

Acquisitions

At some period in your life, you may acquire property or cash from an inheritance, a successful business transaction or even a big win on the lottery. This could be the time to make your will to ensure that your assets are disposed of as you would wish.

Risks

You may embark upon some form of risky activity such as sky-diving, take a job which carries a high risk of injury or illness, travel frequently by air or make visits to 'dangerous' places. These could be good reasons for making your will.

In conclusion there is no time like the present to make your will.*

* *A properly made will reduces the stress on those you leave behind.*

The benefits of making a will

When a person dies, they usually leave behind grieving relatives and friends. The last thing such people want to do at such a difficult time is to have to sort out your estate because you did not leave a will.

Here are some good reasons for making a will:

~ to make life simpler for those you leave behind

~ to ensure that your estate goes to the people you want to benefit

~ to ensure that your spouse is not deprived of his or her home

~ to ensure that a common law partner benefits as you would wish

~ to ensure that funeral expenses are paid from your estate

~ to ensure that your estate does not go to unknown relatives

~ to minimise the tax on your estate

~ to ensure that your assets are properly managed

~ to help your affairs to be settled quickly

~ to give you and your family peace of mind

~ to ensure that any changes in circumstances do not accidentally revoke your wishes.

What happens if you do not make a will

Although the making of a will is a comparatively simple matter, almost two-thirds of the people in the United Kingdom die without making one. There are several reasons for this:

~ Many people believe that their estate will automatically go to their spouse when they die.

~ Others have no close relatives or friends and could not care less what happens when they die.

~ A few genuinely have nothing to leave.

~ Some believe that only rich people make wills.

~ The majority, however, have 'just not got round to making one'.

Any person who dies without making a will is said to have died *intestate*. In such cases their estate is subject to the laws of intestacy and the estate will be disposed of according to predetermined rules.*

The rules of intestacy

These laws or rules were drawn up in 1925 and are somewhat outdated as they do not take into consideration the changes that have taken place in family relationships in recent years. Nevertheless, they still apply and the only things that have altered are the sums of money involved.

The rules of intestacy include a set order in which relatives can benefit from the estate. This is:

* *If you die without making a will there is a chance that your estate may not go to the people you wish to benefit.*

~ spouse (legally married husband or wife)

~ children (including illegitimate and adopted ones but not step-children)

~ parents

~ brothers and sisters

~ half-brothers and half-sisters

~ grandparents

~ uncles and aunts (full blood)

~ uncles and aunts (half blood).

If any of the above die before you, then their children, if any, will benefit.*

There are certain conditions that apply to the distribution of an estate under the rules of intestacy:

~ All funeral and other costs must be settled first.

~ If the spouse is living and there are no surviving children, parents, brothers, sisters, nephews or nieces, the spouse will receive the entire estate.

* *The intestacy laws are archaic and do not take into account current changes in people's relationships.*

~ If both the spouse and children are living, the spouse will be entitled to all personal items, the first £125,000, plus a life interest in half the remainder or residue of the estate. The other half goes to the children who will also receive the first half on the death of the surviving spouse.

~ If the spouse is living and there are no children but there are parents, brothers or sisters (and/or their children), the spouse will be entitled to the first £200,000 together with half of the residue, with the other half going to the parents and then equally to brothers and sisters.

~ If there is no surviving spouse but there are children, the estate will be divided equally between them upon their reaching the age of 18 or marrying, whichever occurs first.

~ Where there is no surviving spouse or children, the estate will go in equal shares according to the above list – i.e. if one or more parent is alive, they will receive the estate, then brothers and sisters and so on.

The law states that the surviving spouse is entitled to continue living in the matrimonial home until his or her death.

All property, bank and savings accounts and other assets owned jointly are automatically transferred to the surviving owners. So, even if you don't have a will, you should make sure that at least your home is jointly owned with your spouse.

Problems caused by not making a will

Dying intestate can cause numerous problems, particularly to the surviving relatives.

~ If there is no will, there will be no executors, therefore members of the family will have to deal with the matter.

~ It will take more time to deal with the estate than if there had been a will.

~ All bank and building society accounts will be frozen (unless held in joint names) until probate (authorisation) is granted. During this time the surviving spouse may have insufficient funds to live on.

~ If there are no surviving close relatives, it may be necessary to engage the services of a solicitor to locate distant relatives. This will not only cost money but could result in the estate being inherited by a distant relative that the deceased person has not seen for many years or even did not know existed.

~ A divorced person is no longer considered to be a spouse from the date of the decree absolute and therefore has no claim on the estate.

~ If a separation order has been granted by a Divorce Court, the above applies. However, if such an order is granted by a Magistrates Court then the surviving spouse can claim as a normal spouse under the rules of intestacy.

~ Although a couple may have lived together for many years, if one of them dies intestate, the partner has no claim under the law. However, they can make a claim, through the Inheritance (Provision for

Family and Dependents) Act 1975 (see Chapter 4).*

All of the above problems can be avoided simply by making a will.

Summary points

★ Ease your family's problems on your death by making a will.

★ Remember that you can change your will at any time.

★ Make a will even if you intend leaving everything to your spouse.

★ Avoid the problems caused by intestacy.

★ Give yourself and your family peace of mind by making a will.

* Dying intestate can prove to be very expensive.

2 Writing a Will

Making a will is a comparatively simple matter. It is the right and duty of every eligible person to make one.

In this chapter, six things that really matter:
~ What can be included in your will
~ Who can benefit from your will
~ Methods of making a will
~ Who is involved
~ Constructing the will
~ Legal requirements

Before actually making your will it is important to take time to plan it properly. First of all, work out what you want to leave and to whom. The next thing is to decide whether to write the will yourself or seek legal advice. Finally, make sure that your will meets all the legal requirements to ensure that it is valid.

What can be included in your will

As the purpose of a will is to ensure that your wishes are honoured on your death, you can include whatever you like as long as it is legal.

Cash

Also known as pecuniary legacies, this includes all amounts held in current and savings accounts in banks, building societies and other financial institutions. It is worth remembering that any money left as a gift can be retrieved to pay off outstanding debts.

Property

This includes all land and buildings owned solely by the deceased. Any property held in joint names as beneficial joint tenants will automatically pass to the other joint owner(s) and you are not entitled to dispose of your share in any other way. If, however, the joint owners die before you then you become the sole owner and can dispose of the property as you wish. The bequest of buildings normally includes the land on which they stand. The only exception to this is agricultural land, where specific fields could be left to other people.

It is also possible to leave leasehold property to others, although in some cases it may be necessary to obtain the permission of the owner before assigning the lease.

Shares

These can be disposed of in the same way as other assets, although there would be restrictions on shares held in a private company. It may be a condition that the shareholders in a private company have the right to decide who can hold shares and any such shares must be offered for purchase to the remaining shareholders.

Insurance policies

Unless the terms of any policy restrict who can benefit upon your death, or it is held as equity against a loan, you can leave the amount due on your death to whom you wish.

Personal items

Any items that you own, such as jewellery, books, vehicles and so on, can be bequeathed as you wish. It is advisable to identify each item in your will. For example, 'I leave my diamond engagement ring to my daughter Mary Jones'. This will prevent any such items from being seized to pay off any outstanding debts.

Trusts

Trusts can be set up as part of the will for the benefit of individuals, particularly beneficiaries under the age of 18 at the time of your death, or for charitable purposes. As trusts can be complex, it is advisable to take professional advice if you intend setting up a trust.

Future income

There are circumstances where you may be entitled to receive a continuing income after your death. A typical example of this is royalties for any books that you may have written. You will therefore need to name one or more people who will be entitled to this income, or you may decide to set up a trust to manage this income on behalf of an individual or charity.

Funeral details

Your will can contain details of how you wish your funeral to be arranged, the type of service, whether you want to be buried or cremated and so on. If you wish your body to be left to medical science or your organs to be donated, this must be made known to the appropriate people well before your death.*

Who can benefit from your will

You can, of course, leave gifts in your will to whomever you wish. However, to avoid any possible confusion or misunderstandings, here are a few points to consider.

Adults

Anyone over the age of 18 is considered to be an adult. To avoid any misinterpretation, it is wise to name each person rather than

* *You can leave virtually anything that you own in your will.*

simply their relationship to you. For example, 'I leave the sum of £500 to my cousin Robert Smith.'

If a person named in your will dies before you do, that gift becomes part of the residue of your estate. Therefore you should make provision for this by naming another person who will benefit should that happen. When a bequest is made to your children or any other direct descendants, if they die before you, the gift will automatically go to their children unless you direct otherwise in your will.

Bankruptcy

It is worth remembering that should a beneficiary be a declared bankrupt or threatened with bankruptcy, there is a risk that the gift could end up in the hands of that person's creditors. To prevent this, you can set up a protective trust which will allow the beneficiary to enjoy the interest from the gift for the period of the trust. When that time expires, the trustees can distribute the gift at their discretion, ensuring that no creditor would benefit.

Witnesses

It is important to remember that witnesses to your will are **not entitled** to benefit from your will. There are three exceptions to this: if the gift is in payment of a debt owed to a witness; if one or more witnesses are also named as trustees, in which case they are entitled to reasonable expenses; if the witnesses have only witnessed a codicil or addendum that does not affect them.

Children

You may leave gifts to your children including illegitimate and adopted ones. Should you have step-children to whom you wish to leave a bequest, they must be identified as such in the will. It is important to remember that anyone under the age of 18 may not legally own buildings or land. It is therefore usual to set up a trust to take care of such gifts until the beneficiary reaches 18.*

Recent developments in areas such as fertilization treatments, genetic engineering and surrogacy have created a potential legal

* To avoid any confusion, clearly name your beneficiaries in the will and not simply their relationship to you.

minefield regarding inheritancy. Currently this
matter is covered by the Human Fertilisation
and Embryology Act 1990. It is advisable for
any executor who is aware of or suspects the
existence of such a situation to consult a
solicitor specialising in this aspect of the law.
With increasing scientific developments, the
legal problems are likely to become even
more complex.

Foreigners

The only restriction to other nationals
receiving gifts from your will is if their
country is at war with yours or that person is
residing in an enemy country. In this case
they may only receive any gifts once peace
has been declared.

Animals

You may leave money for the care of pets or
any other animals for a time limit of 21 years.

Charities

The majority of charities are well organised to
receive gifts from people's wills. Should you

wish to make a bequest to one or more charities you would be advised to obtain the relevant information from those charities, as there are considerable tax concessions to be gained. If the charity you choose is very small or obscure, make provision in your will for that gift to be used for charitable purposes in case your selected charity no longer exists at the time of your death.

Methods of making a will

There are three ways of making a will.

Do-it-yourself

You may decide to make your will yourself. It can be written on a plain piece of paper – or any other material for that matter. You can also purchase a will-making kit from most major stationers which will also include basic instructions. If you choose to use this method it is vitally important to ensure that the wording is correct to avoid any future misunderstandings.

Your will can be handwritten or typed or a

mixture of both. If it is handwritten then make sure that it is legible. It can be written in ink or pencil but not a combination of both. If it is written in both, the parts written in pencil will be considered to be alterations or additions and will be ignored.*

Solicitors

It is advisable to use the services of a solicitor for even the simplest of wills. They can give you appropriate advice and have the experience to word the will to avoid future problems. Solicitors tend to use archaic terms and phrases, the reason being that such terms, through constant use over many years, are universally accepted and understood in law. In the interests of clarity, apart from beginning sentences with capital letters and ending them with full stops, solicitors do not use punctuation. Incorrect punctuation can lead to difficulties in interpreting intent. Solicitors normally charged around £60 for writing a simple will. They will also hold the original or a copy on your behalf at no extra cost.

* Remember, to be legally valid, your will must be signed and dated by you in the presence of two witnesses, who must also sign the will.

Will writing agencies

The reputable ones provide a similar service to solicitors and usually come to your home to prepare the will. Although they should be well versed in writing wills, they will not necessarily have a legal qualification. Their fees vary from £25 upwards and they will normally charge for holding a copy of the will.*

Who is involved

To clarify who is involved in the making of a will, here is an explanatory list:

~ **Testator** – This is the term used for the person making the will. There can be only one testator for each will, therefore a husband and wife will need to make separate wills.

~ **Beneficiaries** – These are the people who will benefit from the will. They should be clearly identified by name to avoid any confusion. For example, 'my brother David Smith', 'my friend Maureen Green'.

* *If you intend to write your own will, make sure you get the wording right. It is far safer to have it made professionally.*

~ **Witnesses** – To be legally valid, your will
must be signed and dated by you in the
presence of two witnesses, who must also
sign the will. As previously mentioned, with
few exceptions, witnesses cannot be
beneficiaries. If it is later discovered that
you have left a gift to a witness, they will
not be entitled to receive it and the gift
becomes subject to the rules of intestacy.

~ **Executors** – You will need to appoint one
or more people to act as executors of your
will. Their function is to administer your
will upon your death and ensure that your
wishes are carried out correctly. Anyone
over the age of 18 can be an executor, but
before appointing them, make sure that
they are willing to act on your behalf.
Unlike witnesses, executors can also be
beneficiaries. If your will is complicated,
you may decide to appoint professional
executors such as your solicitor or bank.
They will make a charge for this service
according to a scale of fees. Provision for
this needs to be included in your will.

~ **Trustees** – The duty of a trustee is to

manage trusts set up in your will. Anyone over the age of 18 can be a trustee, including executors and witnesses. However, you will need to obtain their agreement before appointing them as their duties could continue for many years after your death. They are obliged to manage the trust in the best possible way, which could include investing money to obtain the best return. You can of course appoint professional trustees but remember that they will charge for their services.*

Apart from any gifts that you may leave them in your will, non-professional executors and trustees can claim expenses for administering your will.

Constructing the will

As previously mentioned, you are free to write your will in any way that you wish. It can be on any material, preferably paper and written in ink or pencil, typed, or prepared on a word processor or PC as long as there is 'hard copy' that can be signed by you and your

* *You can leave gifts to your executors and trustees but not to your witnesses.*

witnesses. However, to ensure that your will is legally valid and not subject to misinterpretations, it is vitally important to make sure that the wording is clear and without any ambiguities. Remember, when the time comes to administer your will, you will not be around to clarify any points or misunderstandings. There are minimum legal requirements which, if not met by your will, could result in it being rejected and your estate being dealt with as if no will had been made.

To simplify the writing of your will, you can use 'statutory will forms'. These are legal documents expressing your general intentions and can be referred to in your will. An example is 'Form 2', which enables you to give all your personal possessions to an individual beneficiary without having to list every item. You would simply refer to 'Form 2 of the Statutory Will Forms 1925'.*

* *Keep your will as simple as possible to prevent any misunderstandings. Remember you will not be there to sort out any problems.*

The following list can be used to make sure that nothing essential or important is omitted from your will.

~ Begin by stating that this is your last will and testament.

~ Include your full names and address and the date you are writing the will.

~ Include a statement revoking all previous wills, if applicable.

~ Name your executors and trustees together with an provision for payment for their services.

~ Include instructions as to your funeral and disposal of your body.

~ You may wish to express your thanks and gratitude to people not included in your bequests.

~ Give full details of the disposal of your estate. Remember to name each beneficiary, not simply their relationship or friendship to you. Itemise each gift, unless using statutory will forms.

~ Name a beneficiary for any residue from your estate after all specific gifts have been made.

~ Finally you must sign your will in the presence of two witnesses who must also sign acknowledging that they can verify your signature. Some solicitors suggest that you sign at the bottom of each page of your will as a safeguard against any possible tampering in the future.

Thirty day clause

In the unlikely event that your main beneficiary, such as your spouse, should die within 30 days of your death, it could mean that the gifts that you made to that person would pass to others, contrary to your wishes. To prevent this happening, you can make a provision in your will, stipulating another beneficiary should your main beneficiary not survive you beyond the 30 day period.

Legal requirements

Although there is considerable flexibility allowed when making a will, in order ~~for~~ it to be deemed valid, there are certain legal requirements.

~ It must contain the testator's full name and address at the time of writing the will.

~ It must contain the date on which the will was prepared.

~ It must state that it is your last will and testament.

~ It must contain the names of your executors and trustee if applicable.

~ It must be signed by the testator.

~ It must be signed by two independent witnesses at the same time as being signed by the testator.

~ The testator must be 'of sound mind' when making the will.

~ The testator must be 18 years or age or over when writing the will.

If a person is unable to write for whatever reason, such as physical infirmity or illiteracy, a will can be written by someone else on their behalf and even signed by them. In such a case, a statement must be included at the end of the will stating that the will has been read to the testator and that they are fully aware of and agree with the contents. The will must also of course be signed by two witnesses.*

Summary points

★ Consider using the services of a solicitor to help write your will.

★ Make sure your executors are willing and able to act for you.

★ Remember, under normal circumstances, your witnesses cannot benefit from your will.

★ Keep your will as simple as possible.

★ To ensure that your will is valid, remember the legal requirements.

* An incorrectly written will may be considered invalid in law and the estate become subject to the rules of intestacy.

3 Reducing the Tax Burden

Even death does not mean that you can escape the clutches of the Inland Revenue.

In this chapter, five things that really matter:
~ Inheritance tax
~ Property and other assets
~ Gifts
~ Trusts
~ Paying inheritance tax

A major concern of many people is how much of their estate will go in taxes once they have died. This will of course depend upon the value of the estate. There are however, legal and acceptable ways of reducing the total amount upon which tax is payable.

Inheritance tax

Inheritance tax has replaced estate or death duties and the Capital Transfer Tax. Two bands of taxation are applied to the value of the estate and these are set by the government of the day. The current bands (2000–2001) are:

The first £234,000	Nil
The residue	40%

Thus if someone leaves an estate valued at £500,000, the tax payable will be 40% of £266,000, i.e. £106,400.*

However, by making gifts and other provisions, the person making their will can reduce the value of their estate and so reduce the tax payable. In a great many instances, no tax is payable.

Property and other assets

Property

* Check the current tax bands before making your will.

For most people, their home is their most valuable asset. The tax due will depend on how the property is owned.

Sole ownership – If upon their death the person is the sole owner of a property, the value of the property will be included in the total value of the estate.

Joint tenancy – Property held in joint tenancy with two or more named people, will upon the death of one 'tenant', automatically be owned by the surviving tenants and the value of the property is ignored for tax purposes. It is wise therefore to ensure that your family home is held in joint tenancy with your spouse as this will reduce the total value of your estate. If you own other property, such as a holiday home, make sure that this is also held in joint tenancy.

Tenancy in common – Where a property is held as a tenancy in common with two or more people, each person will own a defined proportion or percentage of the property. When one of the 'tenants' dies, the value of their proportion of the property will be included for inheritance tax purposes. Thus, if a person owns one third of a property valued at £150,000 on their death, £50,000 will be added to the value of their estate. This type of ownership often occurs when several people own properties for the purpose of renting them to others.*

Other assets

Bank and savings accounts – All bank and other savings accounts which are held as joint accounts become the property of the surviving account holders upon the death of one of them. As with property, the value of these accounts do not form part of the taxable value of the estate.

Insurance policies – In order that there will be sufficient money available on your death to at least pay for your funeral and other expenses, it is advisable to take out some form of life insurance. Make sure that the policy includes named beneficiaries, otherwise the sums due will be included in the value of the estate. By making these provisions, you can ensure that the tax due can be substantially reduced or eliminated altogether.

For example, a man dies whilst living with

* *Make sure that your home and other property is owned in such a way that its value is excluded from your estate.*

his wife in a house worth £200,000. He also has bank and savings accounts of £50,000, a life insurance policy upon which £100,000 is payable on his death and other assets such as shares valued at a further £75,000. The face value of his estate is therefore £425,000. However, the house is held in joint tenancy with his wife, the bank and savings accounts in joint names with his wife who is also the named beneficiary on the insurance policy. This leaves an estate valued at £75,000, which is well below the required tax band. In this case no inheritance tax will be due.

Gifts

A popular means of reducing the value of one's estate is by making gifts during one's lifetime. All gifts made at least seven years before death are exempt from tax. Unfortunately, we are not given a seven-year warning of our impending demise. Gifts made less than seven years before death are taxed at 20% according to the following sliding scale:

Years	0–3	3–4	4–5	5–6	6–7
% of charge	100	80	60	40	20

If a gift of £5000 was made in the fifth year before death, the 20% tax would be levied on 40% of £5000, meaning that tax of £400 would be payable on that gift.*

When a gift becomes liable for tax, the recipient is responsible for the payment. If such tax is not paid within 12 months, the deceased person's 'personal representative' – usually the executors – become liable, which can be very embarrassing for all concerned.

However, such gifts can be made 'free of tax', in which case any tax due is paid from the estate.

Exemptions

There are a number of exemptions which mean that no tax is payable. These include:

~ unlimited amounts to your spouse

~ a total of £3000 in any one tax year to any number of people

* *When making a gift before your death, remember to advise the recipient that they could be liable for tax if you die within seven years.*

~ small gifts of up to £250 per person in any one tax year

~ Wedding gifts – up to £5000 per child
up to £2500 per grandchild or other relative
up to £1000 per other person

~ maintenance gifts made to your spouse or ex-spouse, your children or dependent relatives. Children include adopted, illegitimate and step-children up to the age of 18 or until the completion of full-time education, whichever is the longer. Dependent relatives include the aged and infirm who need financial support

~ unlimited sums to registered charities

~ unlimited sums to National Heritage organisations

~ unlimited sums to political parties, although this must not exceed £100,000 in the year before death

~ gifts of business property or shares may

receive up to 100% tax relief. It is important to take legal advice in these matters.

Care must be taken when making gifts, for if it is considered that the donor is continuing to benefit from the gift, its value may be added to the estate. For example, if a person gifts his house to someone else but continues to live there until he dies, the value of the house could be included for tax purposes.

Deed of Variation

If a person receives a gift from a will on which inheritance tax is due, they can, within a two-year period of the testator's death, make a Deed of Variation. Under this Deed, they can redirect, disclaim or give the gift to another person. Tax is then only payable under the terms of this new condition.

For example, a relative may receive a gift upon which tax is due. They can then make a Deed of Variation in favour of the testator's spouse, in which case the tax liability is removed as gifts to spouses are not taxable. Such a Deed must be in writing, signed by

the beneficiary concerned and sent to the
Capital Taxes Office. Of course a Deed can be
refused by the executors if it increases the tax
liability elsewhere and there are insufficient
funds in the estate to pay the increase.

Trusts

A trust is a device whereby a testator can
appoint one or more people, known as
trustees, to manage property or other assets
on behalf of the beneficiary. Trustees may
gain no personal benefit from the gift but
they do have the authority to increase its
value. If, for example, the gift consists of
money, they can invest it and pass the
interest to the beneficiary.*

There are several reasons for setting up a
trust:

~ Where the beneficiary is a minor, a trust
  can be established until they reach a
  specific age – 18, 21 or 25, for example. As
  minors are unable to own land or buildings
  until they are 18, it will be necessary to set

* *Appoint
professional
trustees for all but
the simplest of
trusts.*

up a trust to manage such a gift.

~ If the beneficiary is a bankrupt, the legacy
  could end up with his or her creditors. To
  avoid this, a **protective trust** can be set
  up for a specific period of time during
  which the beneficiary can enjoy the
  interest from the gift. At the end of the
  stipulated time, the trustees can distribute
  the gift at their discretion depending upon
  the circumstances prevailing at that time.
  This type of trust can also be used where
  the testator believes that the beneficiary
  may misuse the gift.

~ Many trusts are established as a means of
  avoiding inheritance tax. For example, a
  main might leave his estate in trust to his
  wife and children, giving his wife a life
  interest in the estate. When she dies the
  estate will pass to the children without any
  tax burden.

~ A trust can be established so that named
  persons or a charity will receive interest
  from the gift for a period of time.

As the role of a trustee is a very important

one, they must be chosen very carefully and of course with their permission. It should be someone in which you have complete confidence. It is always wise to appoint at least two trustees in case one dies before the termination of the trust. If the beneficiary does not believe that the trustees are acting in his or her best interest, they can apply to the court to have the trust terminated. In some cases the trustees can be held liable for any reduction in the value of the gift as a result of their mismanagement.

A trust must be set up for a predetermined time, either a number of years or until a specific event takes place such as the death of a beneficiary. As the setting up of a trust can be a very complex matter, you would be well advised to take professional legal advice before attempting to do so.

Paying inheritance tax

Even after making all possible provisions for reducing the inheritance tax, there may still be an amount of tax to be paid.

The tax due will depend upon:

~ the assessed value of your estate

~ the value of gifts made in the seven years prior to your death

~ the value of exempt gifts made in your will.

As in life, so in death, the Inland Revenue is first in the queue when it comes to pay-outs. Once the estate has been valued and probate has been granted, all inheritance tax must be paid before any other bequests in the will. It may be that property has to be sold in order to meet these payments. In some cases, at the time when the tax is due the value of the estate is an estimate rather than an actual value, particularly where property is waiting to be sold. If the price received is less than the estimated value, the tax paid will be adjusted and the estate will be reimbursed accordingly with interest.

In some cases, the tax can be paid in instalments, normally over ten years. This can eliminate the need for beneficiaries to sell property left to them in order to meet the tax liability. However, interest is payable on the instalments. It is advisable to seek professional advice regarding this method of payment.

Summary points

★ Make sure that your home and other property is held in joint tenancy.

★ Have joint bank and savings accounts.

★ Take out life insurance with named beneficiaries.

★ Donate gifts during your lifetime to reduce or eliminate the need to pay tax.

★ Try to keep the value of your estate below the prevailing tax band.

★ Take legal advice before attempting to establish a trust.

Changing Your Will

You can change your will at any time. Your will can also be changed by the courts after your death.

In this chapter, five things that really matter:
~ Reasons for making changes
~ Making changes to your will
~ Challenging your will
~ Conditions
~ Disputes

Having written your will, do not put it away and forget about it. Your circumstances may change, which could mean that it is not possible to carry out your original intentions. Similarly, after your death your will could be challenged by others resulting in intervention by the courts who may order changes to be made.

Reasons for making changes

There are a number of reasons why it may become necessary to change your will.

Divorce – This invalidates any benefits to a former spouse within the existing will. If you wish to make some provision to him or her when you die, you need to include this in your will.

Marriage – When you marry, any will that you have previously made becomes invalid and you will need to write a new one.

Children – After you have made a will, you may acquire children either naturally, by adoption or as step-children. If you wish to make specific gifts to them, you will need to change your will accordingly.

Grandchildren – This is similar to the above.

Death – Should an original beneficiary die before you do, unless you have already made provision for this in your will, it will be necessary to name another person to inherit that gift.

Change in assets – Since making your will you may have acquired additional assets or disposed of some original ones. You will need to make changes in your will to reflect this.

Change of mind – You may decide for whatever reason to disinherit an original beneficiary and leave that bequest to someone else.*

Making changes to your will

Do not attempt to make changes by writing on or crossing out anything on your original will as this could invalidate the entire will. You can change your will by making additions or supplements to the original will. These are known as *codicils*. A codicil must be written on a separate sheet of paper and signed and witnessed in the same way as the will. Although a correctly drafted codicil has the same legal validity as the will, there could be complications in interpretation. It is always advisable to make a completely new will. When you do so, make sure that you destroy the original will together with all copies. The law

* *It is important to change your will if your personal circumstances alter, otherwise it may be invalid.*

states that when destroying a will, preferably by burning it, it must be intentional and not accidental. Should the original will be accidentally lost or destroyed, a copy is normally accepted as evidence that the original existed.

A codicil must not be stapled or attached to the original will in any way. Thus there is always a chance of it becoming separated and lost. This is another reason for rewriting your will.

Challenging your will

Whilst in theory you can leave what you like to whom you wish, this is not quite true in practice. You would be expected to leave adequate provision to your spouse and any dependent children. Should anyone believe that they are entitled to more than they have been left in the will, they can challenge the will in the courts.*

* If a man dies and leaves £5000 to his wife and £100,000 to a donkey sanctuary, she is quite entitled to challenge the will and is likely to receive sympathy from the court.

Who may challenge

Although anyone can make a challenge, it is normally confined to the following:

Spouse – can make a full claim.

Ex-spouse – can claim for maintenance, particularly if he or she was receiving alimony payments and has not remarried. The exception is if the divorce or legal separation took place within one year of the death, when a full claim can be made.

Children – can claim for maintenance, especially if they were dependent upon the deceased at the time of death.

Step-children – as for children.

Live-in partner – a partner who has lived with the deceased for at least two years immediately prior to the death may also claim. However, the claimant and the deceased must be of opposite sexes as currently the law does not recognise gay relationships.

Other dependents – anyone who was dependent upon the deceased at the time of their death, such as a common law partner or aged parent, can claim for maintenance.*

A will can also be challenged if it is suspected

* Reduce the chances of your will being challenged by taking legal advice before writing it.

that the testator was mentally impaired or under duress at the time of making the will. However, this is often difficult to prove as it places suspicion on other people involved, such as the witnesses, or a solicitor.

In order for any claim to be successful, there must of course be something in the estate to claim against.

Conditions

It is quite acceptable to place conditions on the beneficiaries before they can inherit. However, such conditions may be deemed to be unreasonable in law.

Reasonable conditions

~ Children or grandchildren must reach a certain age before they can benefit as long as the age is reasonable and not punitive.

~ Money can only be used for a specific purpose such as to pay for a university education.

~ Allow children to live at home until they

reach a certain age. Again the age has to be
reasonable. This condition may be difficult
to enforce. If, for example, your children
aged 10 and 12 were living with your ex-
spouse at the time of your death and you
imposed a condition that she must allow
them to live with her until they reached the
age of 21, it would be virtually impossible
to retrieve any gift made to her if she made
them leave home when they were 18.

Unreasonable conditions

Some conditions may be considered
'unreasonable' and can be challenged in the
courts. If the courts agree with the challenger,
the beneficiary will inherit without complying
with the condition. Each challenge is judged
on the facts and circumstances.

The following conditions would normally
be considered to be unreasonable:

~ Not to marry or remarry – either for an
  unreasonable length of time or to a named
  individual.

~ Induce the break-up of a marriage – if the
  condition was that the beneficiary must

divorce his or her partner within say three years.

~ Separating children from parents – this only applies to dependent children, usually minors.

~ Remain celibate – unless the person was already practising celibacy, such as a Roman Catholic priest or member of a religious order.

~ Religious practice – requiring the beneficiary to convert to and practise another religion or sect. It is the practice which would be consider unreasonable and not the conversion.

~ Perform an unlawful act, however minor it may be.

~ Unclear conditions which could have different interpretations such as 'to take care of' an aged uncle.

* If you make your will through a solicitor, they will advise you of any conditions which could be deemed unreasonable.

~ Other conditions such as 'always to live in a certain town' or 'never to visit named countries' would normally be considered unreasonable.*

Disputes

Even though one makes a will which is
apparently clear and concise, it may not
prevent disputes arising over the actual
administration. In many cases it can prove
very costly to resolve disputes, particularly
when solicitors and barristers are involved.

There is the case of the man who died
leaving his entire estate to be equally divided
between his five brothers and sisters. One of
the brothers had died previously, leaving his
share to his two adult children. The value of
the estate was approximately £200,000 and,
apart from a small amount of cash, consisted
of the property in which he had lived. The
dispute arose when two brothers and a sister
wanted to sell the property and divide the
proceeds while the other sister and both
children preferred to rent out the property
and divide the income. The dispute dragged
on for several years involving lawyers and
several visits to court. Eventually the property
had to be sold to pay the costs and each
beneficiary ended up with some £5,000.

If the testator had stated in his will how

the property was to be handled, this very expensive dispute would have been avoided. So the lesson is to make everything in your will as clear as possible to avoid the possibility of any such problems. This is particularly important when it comes to the disposal of assets such as property, shares and items of value.

Summary points

★ Make adequate provisions for your dependents.

★ Changes in your circumstances may require changes to your will.

★ Review your will at least every three years.

★ It is usually simpler to make a new will than to write codicils.

★ Take legal advice before imposing conditions.

★ Avoid disputes by making your intentions as clear as possible in your will.

Understanding Probate

*It is necessary to obtain probate before certain
wills can be administered.*

In this chapter, three things that really matter:
~ The need for probate
~ How to apply for probate
~ The exectuors' duties

Under normal circumstances, probate is
only required where large sums of
money or valuable assets such as property are
involved. If you are responsible for
administering a will and are unsure of the
necessity of obtaining probate, it is wise to
obtain legal advice.

The need for probate

Probate is simply proof or confirmation that
whoever has been appointed to administer the

estate of the deceased has the power to do so. A Grant of Representation will be awarded, which enables those dealing with the will to obtain the necessary documents and financial information. If there is no will or executors, it will be necessary to obtain Letters of Administration by a similar procedure.

The law states three reasons for probate:

~ to make sure that provision is made for the deceased person's dependents

~ to ensure that the estate is distributed according to the deceased person's known or intended wishes

~ to enable any of the deceased's creditors to receive what they are owed as far as possible.

A Grant of Representation or Letters of Administration may be necessary to gain access to any money held by banks, post office, building societies or other financial institutions such as insurance companies. Where the sums involved are small, these bodies will normally release the money without the above documents, although they are not obliged to do so.

How to apply for probate

Who can apply?
~ Any of the executors named in the will can apply.

~ In the case of a will but no named executors, the main beneficiary can apply.

~ If there is no will, application can be made by the following in order:
   - the spouse
   - a child, including an illegitimate one, over the age of 18
   - if all children die before the testator, any of their children over 18
   - a parent
   - a brother or sister
   - any other relative.*

Necessary documents

~ Death Certificate – this will be provided when the death is registered with the local Registrar of Births and Deaths as required

* Your local Probate Office will give you all the help you need to obtain probate.

by law. It is advisable to obtain several copies.

~ The will – make at least one copy in case the original is lost.

Making the application

This is made by the executor through the nearest Probate Registry or Probate Office. If the application is made in writing, it should be to a Registry not an Office.

The procedure is as follows:

1   Send the original Death Certificate and will to the Probate Registry.

2   Complete the following forms, available from the Registry:
    ~   Probate Application Form – PR83
        Details of the deceased, relatives of the deceased, the will and the executors.
    ~   Return of the Whole Estate – CAP44
        Specific details of the estate.
    ~   Inland Revenue Capital Taxes Office – CAP37
        Details of all land and buildings

owned by the deceased.

~ Inland Revenue Capital Taxes Office – CAP40

Valuations of the deceased's stocks, shares and securities.

3 Arrange to attend an interview at the Probate Registry or Office most convenient to the executor. This is simply to clarify any problems arising from the above documents. The executor will be required to confirm that the information given on the forms is correct to the best of his or her knowledge.*

The executors' duties

Before appointing your executors make sure that they know what is involved and that they are prepared to act on your behalf.

The main responsibilities of the executors are to:

~ obtain probate

~ pay creditors

* *The most important information is that relating to inheritance tax. Probate will not be granted until this is paid in full or at least the first instalment has been made.*

~ distribute gifts

~ tie up all loose ends.

Obtain probate

This has been largely covered above. To establish the value of the estate, it will be necessary to list each asset together with its value at the time of death.

Example:

ASSET	VALUE (£)
Property	120,000
Bank accounts	5,000
Savings accounts	10,000
Shares	7,500
Insurance policies	50,000
Car	6,000
Jewellery	4,000
Other assets	2,500
Total	**205,000**

NB. Assets owned jointly, such as property, bank and savings accounts, should not be included as they do not form part of the estate's value. Similarly, insurance policies

with a named beneficiary should also be
excluded.

Pay creditors

Before any gifts can be made, the executors
must endeavour to pay all sums due to the
testator's creditors. Hopefully, the deceased
will have kept records showing what is owed
and to whom. However, it may be necessary
to sort through papers and contact the
creditors to obtain accurate information.
Again, it is sensible to make a list.
Example:

ITEM	AMOUNT (£)	CREDITOR
Funeral	1,250	Brown & Sons
Tax	500	Inland Revenue
Mortgage	10,000	London Mortgage Co.
Bank loan	2,000	A.B.C. Bank PLC
Other loan	1,500	Thomas Green
H.P. Agreements	3,500	X.Y.Z. Ltd
Telephone	100	Telephone company
Gas	30	Gas company
Electricity	50	Electricity company

If there is insufficient cash available to pay all the creditors, it may be necessary to sell other assets to meet the debts. Whilst this is at the discretion of the executors, it is normal practice and courtesy to reach an agreement with the main beneficiaries as to which assets should be sold.

Distribute gifts

Once probate has been granted and all debts paid, the executors are free to distribute gifts as laid down in the will. This is where clear identification of each beneficiary together with the gift they are to receive is essential, as it prevents any disputes or arguments.

Where clauses in the will are unclear, such as 'I leave all my paintings to my children', the executors can act as arbiters and decides which painting can go to which child, although any such decisions are not binding in law.

If the current whereabouts of a beneficiary are unknown, the executors must attempt to find them. This may mean hiring the services to a solicitor who in turn may place a notice in national newspapers asking one or more named persons to contact them. The cost of tracing beneficiaries is borne by the estate of the deceased.

Tie up loose ends

Depending upon individual circumstances, the executors may also be responsible for winding up the estate by:

~ collecting all monies owed to the deceased

~ obtaining rebates on unexpired items such as Road Fund Tax and TV licence

~ cancelling all direct debits and standing orders

~ cancelling any rental agreements

~ cancelling subscriptions

~ contacting the Benefits Agency regarding pensions and other payments

~ contacting the DVLA

~ contacting the utility companies (gas, electricity, telephone)

~ advising clubs, societies and other bodies

to which the deceased belonged

~ redistributing unclaimed or unwanted gifts

~ arranging the sale of property and other assets where there is no identified beneficiary.

Summary points

★ Seek assistance from the Probate Registry.

★ List and value all the assets solely owned by the deceased.

★ Pay all known creditors.

★ Ensure all monies owed to the estate are collected.

★ Distribute gifts according to the will.

★ Resolve disputes to the best of your ability.

★ Attempt to trace all beneficiaries.

★ Finally, check and double check to make sure that nothing has been left unresolved.

Other Types of Wills

In this chapter, five things that really matter:

~ Making a will in Scotland

~ Military wills

~ International wills

~ Living wills

~ Powers of Attorney

A lthough most of the laws relating to wills are applicable throughout the United Kingdom, there are circumstances where they differ.

Making a will in Scotland

The main differences with making a will in Scotland are:

Age – A will can be made by a male aged over 14 and a female over 12.

Marriage – This does not invalidate or revoke an existing will.

Children – It is necessary to specify the

status of any illegitimate or adopted children in the will. Also, if one has children after making the will and they are not mentioned, the will becomes void and a new one is required.

Witnesses – If the will is completely handwritten, it does not require witnesses, however the testator must sign at the bottom of each page. If the will is not completely handwritten, it will need two witnesses who must also sign at the bottom of each page.

Claims – Under Scottish law, the surviving spouse and children have more rights to claim against the estate even if it was the intention of the testator to exclude them. Similarly, other dependents have a reduced claim. For example, a surviving spouse with no children can claim half the estate excluding property. In the case of a spouse with children, the spouse can claim one third of the estate and the children one third between them again excluding property.*

Intestacy – The intestacy laws in Scotland differ considerably from those in the rest of

* *Scottish law only applies if you reside in Scotland when you die. If you die in Scotland but live in England, then English law will apply to your will.*

the United Kingdom.

~ A surviving spouse with no children, parents or other close relatives is entitled to receive the whole estate.

~ In the case of a spouse with children, the spouse is entitled to the property, personal possessions and one third of the remainder. The children then share equally what is left.

~ Where there are children, excluding step-children, but no spouse, the children share the estate equally.

~ Should there be no spouse or children, the parents will take half of the estate and any brothers and sisters share the other half.

~ If none of the above applies, then the following benefit in order:

- full blood uncles and aunts or their children
- half blood uncles and aunts or their children
- grandparents
- full blood great uncles and aunts or

their descendents
- half blood great uncles and aunts or their descendents
- great grandparents.

If none of these people can be found, the Crown can distribute the estate to anyone with a reasonable claim, such as a close friend of the deceased.

Military wills

This only applies to servicemen and servicewomen who die whilst on active service – that is, during a war. Normally, such a will is only made where the person has been seriously wounded and is likely to die.*

~ The will can be written, in which case it does not have to be witnessed.

~ Where it is not possible or practical to have a written will, the intentions of the person making the will can be made verbally to a witness.

~ Witnesses to such wills can also be

* All members of the armed forces are advised to make a will before being posted to 'active' areas.

beneficiaries.

~ There is no minimum age for making a military will.

~ Whether the will was made verbally or in writing, it can be revoked at any time by similar means for as long as that person remains in the armed services.

~ When a person returns to civilian life, they must make a will in the normal way. However, if that person is a minor, they cannot revoke the will until they reach the age of 18.

~ There is no inheritance tax liability on the estate of anyone dying whilst on active service.

As military wills require a great deal of trust on the part of all parties concerned and are open to misinterpretation and abuse, all military personnel are strongly advised to make a normal will before embarking on active service.

International wills

Where a person has property or other assets in several different countries, it is now possible to make one will and have it administered in any country that is party to the agreement. It does not matter where the will was drawn up, where the assets exist or what the nationality or residence of the person making the will is.

There are, however, certain minimum requirements:

~ The will must be in writing but can be in any language.

~ The person making the will must declare in front of a solicitor and two witnesses that it is their will and they are aware of its contents.

~ The testator must sign and number each page of the will in the presence of a solicitor and two witnesses, who must sign the final page of the document.

~ The solicitor must add the date of the signing, which becomes the date of the will.

~ The solicitor must attach a special certificate to the will which gives details of where the will is to be kept.

As this is a comparatively recent innovation, further information about this type of will can be obtained from the Foreign Office or, if abroad, the British Embassy or Consulate.

Living wills

The purpose of a Living Will is to enable a person to express in written form their wishes in certain medical matters. For example, in the event of that person becoming terminally ill, they may request that they do not receive any life-prolonging drugs or other medication. Similarly, should the individual be involved in an accident resulting in them only being kept alive via a life support system, they can request that once their condition has been diagnosed, the system should be switched off.

A Living Will is not a will in the strict sense of the term and should not contain any instructions that would be included in a normal will, as it has no legal validity.*

* A Living Will is completely separate from a normal will. You can have a Living Will without having a will.

Anyone wanting to make a Living Will needs to complete a form setting out their wishes. They must date and sign the form in the presence of a witness who must also add their signature. Whilst being mentally capable, the witness must not be a spouse or anyone else who will benefit from that person's ordinary will.

A Health Care Proxy, often a qualified medical practitioner, can also be appointed and named in the will. This person can be consulted regarding the carrying out of the wishes should the individual concerned not be capable of making any final decisions.

Such wills can of course be altered or revoked at any time.

Powers of attorney

The object of giving power of attorney is to enable someone else to act on your behalf in certain specified matters. The person giving the power is called the *donor* and the one to whom it is granted is known as the *attorney*. Both the donor and the attorney must be over 18, mentally capable and in the case of the attorney must not be an unresolved bankrupt.

There are two types: General Powers of Attorney and Enduring Powers of Attorney.

General powers of attorney

This simply gives the authority for a named individual to act on your behalf in financial and business matters for a specific period of time. For example, if you were to go abroad for several months or years, you could appoint someone that you trust to deal with your affairs, such as paying bills, making business decisions and handling your investments. With the rapid advance in world-wide electronic communication it is becoming less necessary to grant general powers of attorney in such cases. However, it can still be appropriate should you, for example, be hospitalised for a long period of time.

To grant a general power of attorney it is simply a matter of completing the appropriate form as set out by the Power of Attorney Act 1971, giving the name and address of the attorney and detailing the extent of their authority, together with the donor's signature.

Enduring powers of attorney

This enables the attorney to act on behalf of the donor when the latter is no longer mentally capable of acting for themselves. Under the terms of the Enduring Powers of Attorney Act 1985, the appointed attorney must apply to the Court of Protection for permission to act for the donor. Whilst an attorney can deal with all business, financial and most legal matters, he or she cannot:

~ Write a will on behalf of the donor nor alter or amend any existing will.

~ Make any decisions regarding the donor's health, hence the introduction of the Living Will.

~ Influence any changes to the donor's marital status.

~ Appoint his or her successor.

Summary points

★ Wills made in Scotland are subject to Scottish law.

★ Military wills only apply to service people on active service.

★ International wills are valid in every country that is party to the convention.

★ Although currently Living Wills have no legal validity, the government is considering making them as legally binding as normal wills.

★ Before appointing an attorney, particularly one with enduring powers, seek legal advice.

7 And Finally

To simplify the administration of your estate when you die, make sure that your affairs are in order and easily available to your executors.

In this chapter, two things that really matter:
~ Safeguarding your will
~ Keeping records

Safeguarding your will

Having gone to the trouble of making a will, make sure that it is in safe keeping.

If you have made your will through a solicitor, they will keep the original for you at no additional cost. It is sensible to retain a copy and store it in a safe place with your other personal documents.

Keeping records

To help your executors administer your will quickly and efficiently, keep a record of all necessary documents and people to be contacted.

The following lists should be helpful in deciding what information to record.

Personal items

Your will
Birth certificate
Marriage certificate
Divorce licence
Passport
Driving licence
National Insurance number
Social Security number
Tax office and number
Funeral arrangements
Organ donation details

Financial items

Bank accounts
Building society accounts
Post office accounts

Insurance policies
Savings certificates
Premium Bonds
Pension plans
Pension book
Stocks and shares
Other savings
Hire purchase agreements
Rental agreements
Safety deposit boxes
Unpaid bills
Money owed
Property owned
Other valuable assets.

Persons to be contacted

Solicitor
Accountant
Contact at place of work
Insurance broker
Religious adviser
Relatives
Friends
Groups and societies to which you belong.

Although some of the above items may not be applicable and others can be included, remember that when the time comes, you will not be in a position to tell people where things are kept or what other instructions you want carried out.

Summary points

★ File and label all important documents.

★ Keep a list of where everything of importance is stored.

★ Make sure your 'filing system' is up to date.

Appendix 1
Glossary

Here is an explanation of common words and terms used in wills.

Absolute Without any conditions.

Ademption The cancellation or reduction of a gift specified in a will because it is no longer wholly owned by the testator at the time of death.

Administrator A person who is appointed to deal with the affairs of the deceased when there is no will.

Asset Anything owned, such as property, car, jewellery, shares, etc.

Assent A document by which the executors transfer freehold or leasehold property to the beneficiary.

Beneficiary A person or organisation who inherits through a will or intestacy.

Bequest A gift other than land or property.

Chargeable gift Any gift liable for tax.

Children Includes legitimate, illegitimate and legally adopted children.

Codicil An amendment or addition to a will.

Deceased The person who has died.

Descendants Children, grandchildren and in

some instances, nephews and nieces.

Devise To give a gift of property, building or land.

Engrossment The final copy of a legal document.

Estate The total property of the deceased.

Exception estate Where the value of an estate is such that it is not necessary to submit the Inland Revenue Account form.

Executor Someone who is appointed by the testator to administer his/her will.

Free of tax A gift where any tax liable is paid from the estate and not by the beneficiary.

Gift Anything left in a will to a named person or organisation.

Absolute gift – without any conditions

Conditional gift – with specific conditions.

Indenture A deed creating or transferring land.

Infant A person under the age of 18.

IHT Inheritance Tax.

Intestate Dying without a valid will.

Issue Direct blood line descendants.

Joint tenants Two people who own a property jointly, which on the death of one becomes the sole property of the survivor.

Legacy A gift other than a house or land.

Life interest Any gift left to an individual for their lifetime only, such as a house.

Life tenant A named person to enjoy the benefits of a life interest.

Minor Another term for infant.

Next of kin The closest living blood relative.

Pecuniary legacy A gift of money in a will to a named person or organisation.

Probate Document issued by the Probate Registry confirming the validity of the will and authorising the executors to act on behalf of the deceased.

Recital A statement in a will, usually expressing thanks to people who will not benefit from your estate.

Residue What is left from an estate after all gifts and legacies have been made.

Small estate Currently in England and Wales where the gross value is less than £5000.

Survivor The married or unmarried partner alive at the time of the testator's death.

Tenants in common Where two or more

people own specified shares or portions of the property. The value of that portion owned by the deceased is included in the estate for tax purposes.

Testamentary expenses Reasonable costs incurred in administration of the estate.

Testator A deceased person who has made a valid will.

Trusts Assets left for trustees to manage on behalf of beneficiaries are held in trust. These are often set up for infants and tax saving purposes.

Trustees Those people having a legal ownership of the assets in a trust until such time as they are transferred to the beneficiary.

Terms specific to Scottish law

Bond of caution Money set aside to compensate the estate for any loss caused by an executor's errors.

Confirmation A Grant of Probate.

Docket A formal note.

Heritable property Land or buildings.

Legal rights These are the rights of the surviving spouse and/or children to benefit from the estate regardless of the terms of the will or rules of intestacy.

Prior rights Relating in particular to the surviving spouse's rights in cases of intestacy.

Appendix 2
Sample Will

This is a sample of a simple will recently drawn up by a solicitor. Only the names and addresses have been changed.

THIS WILL dated *fifth* day of *June* in the Year Two Thousand is made by me **HENRY JAMES COLE** of 35 Jubilee Drive Devizes Wiltshire

1. **I REVOKE** all former testamentary dispositions
2. **I APPOINT** as my Executors and Trustees **MARY ISOBEL COLE** of 35 Jubilee Drive aforesaid and **JOHN PETER GREEN** of 70 Woodridge Road Melksham Wiltshire AB1 2CD and in this my Will the term "my trustees" shall include the Trustees for the time being of the Will and Trusts arising under it
3. **I GIVE** the sum of FIVE HUNDRED POUNDS (£500) to each of my nephew **DAVID GREEN** and my niece **ANNE GREEN** free of tax absolutely
4. **I GIVE** all my estate both real and personal not hereby or by an Codicil hereto otherwise specifically disposed of unto my Trustees **UPON TRUST** for the

said **MARY ISOBEL COLE** absolutely but if she shall predecease me then for my sister **SUSAN ELIZABETH GREEN** absolutely

5. **ANY** person living at my death who does not survive me by at least one month shall be deemed to have predeceased me for the purpose of ascertaining the devolution of my estate and I DECLARE that any intermediate income shall pass to my Trustees or ultimate Beneficiaries without reference to such person

IN WITNESS whereof I have hereunto set my hand the day and year first written

SIGNED BY THE TESTATOR

In our joint presence and attested

By us in the presence of him and that of each other